FIRST AND LAST MUSIC

With all good wishes
Christine

4th Nov. 2014

FIRST AND LAST MUSIC

CHRISTINE MCNEILL

Shoestring Press

Printed by imprintdigital
Upton Pyne, Exeter
www.imprintdigital.net

Typeset by narrator
www.narrator.me.uk
info@narrator.me.uk

Published by Shoestring Press
19 Devonshire Avenue, Beeston, Nottingham, NG9 1BS
(0115) 925 1827
www.shoestringpress.co.uk

First published 2014
© Copyright: Christine McNeill

The moral right of the author has been asserted.

ISBN 978 1 907356 93 3

ACKNOWLEDGEMENTS

Acknowledgements are due to the following publications where some of the poems, or versions of them, first appeared: *Acumen, Agenda, Dreamcatcher, Reactions, Scintilla.*

for David
with gratitude, as always

CONTENTS

WALTHER VON DER VOGELWEIDE

My bird – bird of the field:
wing splayed where the sun
transforms the frosty grass
into iridescent pearls.

It drinks a drop of melted cold;
head tilted to the warming sun,
beak ajar

as if more might come –
a gift from above.

At times I imagined to live
in the little room of its throat
where it wove a fabric of ardour.

I wandered to Austria,
learned to sing and tell at the Babenberg court –
became the bird's phantom rival.

BUSKER

Slim as a flower
she looks at me from the front page.
I take up the saxophone,
turn to murder, drought,
some far-off mayhem.

Red curtains in a shop-window
and she's there again, trying on lipstick.
That quivering artery as she cranes her neck
for colours higher up the rack,
and I wonder if a butterfly

alighting on that spot
would make her tremble more.
I do a *Little Red Monkey* tune –
her finger speeds to coral-pink
and suddenly I'm beside her,

breathing her perfume
like a whispered prayer.
I'm wearing a white tuxedo,
she an off-the-shoulder dress –
her choice of lipstick

a red waterfall
I long to put my hand in.
I follow her with *The Song of the Rose* –
she walks fast – I do the same.
She runs – and I keep up:

through red curtains
that are sheer lace.
I'm a protecting brother
and a seducing lover; she the kill
walking home beside the hunter.

JOHANN JOSEPH FUX

(Austrian Baroque composer)

I looked for the human in God.
Saw the frailty of life
and my heart wept:
out of this came something so
pure into my ears,
a pious landfall of chords:

sun-turned, rain-tuned –
as distance dissolved
it was as if all birds of the world
were singing at once.
Inventing counterpoint, I became Europe's
musical god; fêted by emperors, by my own heart.

SOUND MEDITATION

Palms open on his lap
invite the listener in.

From his throat
a sound

abandons him
as it draws out

into the church's interior:
man-child, child-spirit –

light
bordering on the infinite.

CHRISTOPH WILLIBALD GLUCK REFLECTS ON MARIE-ANTOINETTE

With sparrow-bone fingers
she pussy-footed on the harpsichord:
my gaze transfixed on her translucent skin.

Afterwards
when she rose,
her steps quickening like gold,

I let the rain play on my soul
and had the feeling it was she
who was complete

and not the music.

Back home, the cat brought in a sparrow.
I stared at the jumble of bones.
My wife poured wine:

she too wanted to be of special service.
It was God's will
and I drank.

INDIAN MINIATURE SEEN THROUGH A MAGNIFYING GLASS WHILE LISTENING TO JOHN TAVENER'S *THE PROTECTING VEIL*

Each painted hair,
each painted flower on her sleeve
as she offers a white cup to drink
is desire

Desire is wine
a cool, cool sip

Desire in his reaching hand
and on his lips

It seems all life
has been squeezed
into the white cup she offers him

Her eyes and lips
pour out an inner repletion

And the life she is losing
he pours back into her gaze

Desire, that he draws from her face,
returns to its hiding-place.

PREPARING FOR BURIAL

This is Haydn
who had given the world *The Creation*,
104 symphonies,
59 divertimenti,
24 piano concertos,
68 string quartets,
20 piano trios,
6 cello concertos,
24 operas,
14 masses,
The Seasons, and much more.

The women who clothe him for eternity,
arranging the hair as they see fit,
do not know that his head will be stolen
from the coffin after burial
by an admirer of his music and follower
of the abstruse study of skulls.
For over a decade the theft will remain undiscovered
before the head comes into the hands
of an anatomist. His heirs
will cherish it for almost a century,
until finally it rejoins the rest of Haydn's bones.

One of the women strokes his cheek.
She has heard *The Creation* in church.
The story of Adam and Eve
meant for Haydn's first love, Therese
who, becoming a nun, called herself
Sister Josepha, in kinship with his
first name.

The woman recalls the tenor
singing Adam: feeding the church
with his sailing timbre.
How the aria turned cold statues
into blossoming spaces.
It is true, she thinks,
the dead open the eyes of the living.

VIOLIN

Removing the silk cloth
that kept me idle,
he takes me into his arms.
Pretending sleep
I open myself
and in giving
dream:

I'm a lady, opening doors,
rushing to the ball in so much heat –

he takes the bow,
my dance begins.

MOZART'S PET STARLING

I see my master work feverishly
by a gorgeous sunset.

Not long ago I memorised
the first five notes of his piano concerto,

to his delight
sang it in perfect pitch.

To me the master is like
a sunbeam piercing the darkest forest.

Listen: the room
so drunk with sound –

and all this
is given to me, a caged bird.

Down in the *Domgasse*
revellers look up,

hearing a wedding in the sky.

MUSIC IN APPLES

On the radio Pinchas Zuckerman
plays a Mozart violin concerto.
Pinchas – stealth, like in *Pink Panther*.

Zuckerman, I say, looking at shrivelled apples.
Sugar is needed, cinnamon, cloves.
I peel and core and slice.

Last night dreamt of a wedding reception:
apricots, peaches, strawberries
rubbed shoulders with ice-cubes in giant buckets.

This morning saw the moon and sun in the sky,
reconciled,
like strawberries and ice.

Pinchas Zuckerman's violin-play
rolls several moods into one as the apples boil.
Spicy aroma scales the walls.

You come into the kitchen.
Pinchas Zuckerman is playing, I say.
You wash your hands. Touch my bare neck.

I let your cold skin shudder mine,
knowing the apples lukewarm
in a bowl with sugar and cream,

and Pinchas Zuckerman earns all the applause.

BEETHOVEN IN HEILIGENSTADT

The waters in *Heiligenstadt* had healed many.
He came, seeking a cure for his deafness.
It did not happen.

Railing against his affliction
he wrote the *Heiligenstädter Testament*,
dashed down the staircase

past the woman sweeping up dead leaves,
into a country lane where flowers sang in his head
and he conducted them:

such wild strokes, to bless the trees, the grasses.

Now, Japanese tourists drift up the narrow staircase,
bow through the low entrance in self-blessing,
and his *Second Symphony* comes from nowhere.

GREEN SYMPHONY

The Finnish forest so large, you painted
canvas after canvas – paths, clearings, lakes;
the many shades of green
as if with each brushstroke
you wanted to own this land.

Loops and circles made me listen
to the call of an elk,
the screech of a flying squirrel,
and somewhere in the echo-chamber of light
the song of birds.

I was gliding on a carpet of pine needles,
heard you whisper *Yes*
and felt the wart on my cheek
beginning to pucker; an itch
as if the tiniest insect

nibbled at the skin
while you painted the long trunks of trees.
Full moons came and went,
but the one on my cheek hung on
until one morning when the moon

had faded into the bleached sky
I found blood on my pillow:
the wart had come off in the night.

SCHUBERT'S DEATH PLACE

Head-phones on,
press a number on a mock keyboard

and *The Shepherd on the Rock*
babbles in your ears.

A soprano, satin-voiced,
climbs towards ghostly
meadow flowers.

Then a chill,
a liquid cold,

before once more the hope of spring:
I will... I will...

His childlike spectacles
look through a larger transparency;

the clarinet fills a deathly hollow.

"O WIE SCHÖN IST DEINE WELT"

Frau Enderling couldn't wait
for the Japanese soprano to audition.
But – what disappointment!
Her unclear diction
as if a dumpling rolled around her gums,
and her teeth – several missing!
Signalling disapproval by shaking
her gold bracelet, Frau Enderling glanced up
at the church roof, summoning
an angel to stop this pitiful sight
of an ugly duckling singing Schubert.

But when the chord lingered on *immortal,*
it rose from the singer's throat
like water sprung from a most pure source,
flooding the church in waves,
wanting to erase the figures of saints,
the Virgin, the cross –
Frau Enderling, gagged in disbelief,
at the end could only applaud.

JOSEFINE LANG ON ANTON BRUCKNER'S MARRIAGE PROPOSAL

I was seventeen, he forty-two.
It wasn't so much the age-difference
as his slovenly appearance
that put me off. True, I came from
the butcher's trade, wasn't myself
elegant or educated.
But he wasn't good-looking;
his black suit shone with grime.
He ate too much, had no conversation,
and his large head seemed to walk by itself.

Once, I listened to his music.
Nothing had prepared me for
such raw emotions.
I hurried home to trim gristle off beef.
A raven perched on a rock,
looking for what nature had slain.
Bruckner's music rang in my ears –
I could not marry him – no.
The raven disappeared in the wind.
I chopped meat off the bone.

SWAN

You love to see me sew.
Is it the neck bending to the task,
like a swan contemplating the concentric motion
of its patch of water?

The needle tests the cloth,
plunges in. I hum a tune;
each stitch
brings up something from the deep.

I knot and cut the thread;
what you see
empties itself
as the quilt comes to rest in my lap.

BRAHMS

Evening meal churning in his stomach,
he trundles off to *The Red Hedgehog*.
Sits and drinks.

Then back to his rocking-chair, glowing
in last sunlight. Shuts his eyes.
Into this semi-conscious state

comes Clara in mourning.
Empathy and love sweep through him
as he watches her

lean against a plinth
on which her husband stands,
a statue.

Book in her right hand,
thumb marking the page,
she lights him up inside:

a slow silent fragment of night.

LULLABY

Sleep, my little babe, sleep, and dream...

of that water tank
with air trapped
forming bubbles below the lid.

That rusty old ship
lying at the bottom
made of wax.

The windows look out
on fists aiming to hurt:
watch sliced from your wrist,

girls mocking your slowness with words.
Cold water rushes in:
keep still

as in your mother's womb:
her *No* that pained
while she stirred boiling jam,

and years later the *No* oozing
from her skeletal frame:
snow fell on spring irises –

Tomorrow, God willing, you will wake again.

HUGO WOLF

From grabbing a shotgun,
aiming at cooing pigeons
and barking dogs,
wanting silence to compose.

From being a fierce critic
of his fellow musicians,
not shying away
from harsh words.

From composing his most
famous song *Der Feuerreiter*:
a dashing young man in red cap
smelling a fire at the distant mill:

riding through fields and gates,
smoke and heat,
being there where it mattered
and meeting his fate:

he lay on his death-bed,
paralysed by pox,
wasting and burning,
surrounded by doctors.

Brave, riding to his grave
four long years.
Time after time the song
reared in his mind

until it collapsed in ash
and went its way over the world:
Rest in peace,
rest in peace, at the mill.

PAGE TURNER

Always beside me,
reading over my shoulder
the score I played;
noting the tension in my neck;

knowing the exact point,
even though I was still
on the last three chords:
cutting across,

and for a split second
I was in her hands;
dependent like a baby
on its mother's breast.

She turned the page.
With hawk's eyes followed every note –
at times it seemed
teased them from my fingers …

*

Playing Chopin
I teased the bad news from her lips:
the chemo that followed,
her thinness, loss of hair.

Every evening I play
without the music making a sound I hear;
my fingers chase their reflection in the black veneer –
wanting to touch, always fleeing.

GUSTAV MAHLER ON THE RAX

"To be out of Vienna, to breathe the clear
   fresh mountain air…"

Where chamois dice with death in the sun;
where gentians point to the sky's good works;
where an eagle gliding over the valley
holds the secret of love;
and children aren't lost or dead
but part of the ache:
standing by the cross
looking out
over hills, fields, woods –
that *ewig, ewig*: the song of the earth.

A WANDERER'S SONG

(after Mahler)

I

I reached into the clothes container,
grabbed bag after bag
looking for shoes, until finally
long white laces appeared.

Scuffed, but the sole serviceable.
I scrutinised it, as I did instructions
on official forms whose language
I only half understood.

The shoe had belonged to someone
in this city. I mentally measured the distance
between *that* life and mine. It was spring.
Nature was budding, but my heart couldn't join in:

the girl I loved
was getting married.
I rummaged for the shoe's partner,
found it, a size bigger:

laces white as lilies.
Perplexed by someone having worn
odd sizes, I tried them on.
It was like entering a house with uneven floors.

I wanted to cry.
The shoes were useless.
The birds shouldn't sing –
spring was done with.

But I bagged the shoes, and as I walked
heartache went with me and I kicked a bin,
sent litter flying along the street where everything
went its own way.

II

Leaving the city I wandered on country paths.
Once more spring opened up. I wore the discarded
shoes, which stones mocked.
The lilac slipped out its scent, the magnolia
stood like a candelabra. It seemed by lifting
my hand I could make nature sing.

Head spinning from the dervish wind
I looked for a bench to sit on;

passed a wren splashing itself free of mites
in a puddle;

passed a low lancet window
from which once a bell was rung
at the point of consecrating
the host during mass;

walked past secrets
furled in the roots of trees;
my thoughts caught in those fighter planes
rupturing the sky's silence –

paused when I saw a leaf
in all that was blossoming
fall.

III

She'll raise a china cup to her lips,
take the smallest of sips,
put it back on the saucer
with its green-leafed motif.

I want to be there,
lift the knife
into the furrows of talk
towards the cake,
hold it too close to a lily
and stamen
smears the blade

while she dabs the corners
of her mouth,
looks at the orange dust,
then at the napkin
stained with her red lipstick

and time slows
as I aim the knife
at her breast.

I go over the scene in my mind:
see her wide-open eyes,

that gull
gliding beneath a blue sky –

and it is I
with a knife in my breast.

IV

Her blue eyes made me take up
this wandering life.
I feared the sky would crash onto fields.
In a pond fish wove unfathomable paths.
I felt wretched with sorrow.

There were trees so tall,
from afar they looked like huge balls.
Their crowns islands of green,
branches reaching out for each other –
in the blustery wind dancing together.

Under a linden tree I fell asleep.
In the morning
its blossom had almost snowed me in.
I touched the frail flowers –
my heart jumped like a bird's.

KINDERTOTENLIEDER

(after Mahler)

I: Mother and child

The things I bought at *Mother and Child*
I've thrown into black bags.
All day I cry. Tear up the books
on how to get better.

Not long ago, trees swayed in the wind
as I pushed and screamed
and the future came.
I thought: It could kill me, this child

that wants my milk.
I stroked its soft cheek;
it found my nipple.
And sucked me in.

I light candle after candle.
Stare at the dripping wax.
Snatch an insect off my leg;
watch it wriggle, until dead.

II: Madness

I pressed the glass so hard,
it cracked in my hand and I bled.
I slashed the bed with a knife,
tore clothes from the wardrobe,
ripped them up.
Made silent phone calls,
stalked young mothers
wishing them dead.
Accused spiders and beetles,
that woman cleaning her window.
Begged forgiveness;
stared at a crimson rose.

III: Spooning the past

Taking the spoon
I look at the food
before putting it
into my mouth;

when I've licked the spoon
I hold it like an open book
or something I've worn for years –
the reflection of my nose, my lips

abandoned and retrieved
as I turn the spoon.
I smile
as though I've seen a little face

come in behind;
as if each step
creates another
somewhere in the room.

Putting down the spoon
I gaze into the mirror
at an open door,
feel the air tingle

as if a tiny hand
were brushing against my face;
each step, invisible, unheard,
but in my memory a birth.

IV: Growing

The day I bought him new shoes
the sun shone and wispy clouds
idled in the sky.

He tried on trainers,
strutted up and down, jumped and hopped,
almost willing his toes to break out.

On and on he walked into the fierce sun,
joining others,
probing new ground.

A movement, like a fish's fin,
eased down my left cheek,
stopped by the corner of my mouth:

a tear.
It's very hot today, the sales assistant said,
handing me a glass of water.

I took it, afraid to drink,
as though it were a deep pool
and I would drown.

V: Moving on

The bunk bed was taken apart.
Next, the desk. One drawer handle
turned up, as if a secret inside
were having a laugh.

The bedside lamp with its yellow shade:
switched on, it glowed like a prayer.

The toys: each one a bell ringing for celebration,
bringing back the moments of playing.

The chair in the corner cried out for its teddy.
A crack in the door-frame where a ball
had been kicked –

and yet the room was so stubbornly at peace.

The bed's angle, dirty socks underneath –
I fixed these random sights into a wordless order,
left the pink feather by the door.

BRIDGING

(After Mahler's Song: "I have lost track of the world")

A bird of prey carries my loss
into the hairnet of mountain peaks.

Who knows if we haven't been banished
into another time?

And the seraphic blue of a jay
slipping into the traceries of branches –

casts a warmth on something that was.

ALEXANDER VON ZEMLINSKY

There was his affair with Alma Schindler
which ended when Mahler proposed.
His own childhood sweetheart spurning him,
he wedded her sister.

There was his witnessing the *ménage à trois*
of his pupil Arnold Schönberg,
whose wife, Zemlinsky's sister Mathilde,
took up with the artist Richard Gerstl.

When Zemlinsky tried to make her see sense
she returned to Schönberg
and Gerstl took his own life,
for which Schönberg blamed Zemlinsky.

Then came Hitler.
Zemlinsky's mother half-Jewish,
he "racially intolerable",
shunned as composer of *degenerate music*.

His compositions never reached the top.
But as conductor he was highly regarded:
bending like a willow to the wind,
or else he would break.

THE CRY

From a clump of reeds
the cry of a creature.
We can't tell whether a bird
or woodland animal is trapped.

We see a heron
statuesque by the water.
The bird's unmoving eye,
the repeated cry

that has now cornered its own distance
and seeded itself in our heads;
we carry it through the rush of wind
along hedged fields,

through our jokes that fall on dung and weeds,
away from country joggers and gleeful children –
we bear it into the dazzling sun,
pleading for something to be done.

ARNOLD SCHÖNBERG'S *VERKLÄRTE NACHT*
AT PAYERBACH

A bridge over a river,
mountains fading into illusory absence.
A full moon chastening the soul.

In this cool bed of air
something in him built.
Obedient to instinct

he linked with an imaginary other:
she was pregnant by another man.
Love a golden fingerprint,

no need to know how it would end.
He came to as early sun
lit the belly of mountains.

A silence his writing hand pushed against.

ARNOLD SCHÖNBERG'S GRAVE AT VIENNA'S *ZENTRALFRIEDHOF*

A giant cube of stone by Fritz Wotruba
                                        leans
touching the grave with one rear corner –

Has the force of what lies beneath
                                    lifted the stone

or the soul's breath almost caused it
                                to topple?

Sunlight streams across the underside

                            further up
creates a shadow-imprint of bare branches –

                            Moses
receiving the stirrings of the First Commandment

HEREAFTER

This house is not your own.
The rooms defeat you at a glance.
A garden through a glass door:
spindly trees, curving hedges –
this house is not your own.

Yet you know its lay-out.
Like one learning to walk again
after an accident, you take halting steps.
Hear someone whisper *You're free to go.*
But there's no one.

Petunias cascade from a tub,
orange begonias align with the blue
of morning glory.
A pigeon coos.
A robin sings.

The cooing stops.
Yet the robin's song continues:
no note the same –
the bird knows the balance
between sound and stillness.

A child says *My ladybird won't fly!*
You want to respond, but have no breath.
Your throat is closed.
This house is yours.
You're not here at all.

ANTON VON WEBERN

Not a Jew. But by studying
Schönberg's music with students,
the chance of a professorship
was wiped out.

No money. A nervous breakdown.

In 1945, the joy at seeing his son back on leave.
Soon after, the news
he had been killed at the front.

Not in Vienna – his place of birth.
But in the lush hills of Mittersill in Salzburgland,
home of his daughter and son-in-law.

No longer war.

What he didn't know:
American military police
had surrounded the house
to trap his son-in-law,
a black marketeer.

Not for a breath of fresh air. But to smoke
away from the children and women
he stepped out of the house.

Not one shot. But three struck him down.

Not the clear blue sky. But the muddy ground.

SPRING

In his Sunday best
he shows off the top hat
decorated with spring flowers,
with ribbons and small fruit,
given to those Austrians
about to serve in the First World War.
Beside him his uniformed comrades, proud,
as if carrying all they have lived to an altar;
not knowing that the ripening fields
in another country will be littered
with dead bodies and that soon
they would be among them.

A homing pigeon is caught in the photo.
I see it flying up the hill, alight on a branch,
swoop away in an arc
as if showing him the slow way up
to where it all ends
for the wider view –

Blinds drawn on the windows at home.
Walls will record his mother's grief.
And somewhere outdoors in minus two
a robin will summon spring:
untroubled by the dying light, it will fire up its throat:
will only stop when the dark is complete.

ALBERN BERG

A flick of his hand at a wasp
on a pot of jam – it stung:
his hand swelled up: the doctor
unable to treat the erupting boils.

Before that:
twelve-tone music condemned as *degenerate art*;
royalties stopped; forced to sell his house,
the inherited villa, the score of *Wozzeck*.

Before that:
Vienna was finally ready to perform *Wozzeck,*
but Richard Strauss, whom he'd honoured
by citing the *Rosenkavalier* waltz-motif,

left the opera after the second act.

Before that:
the death of the young Manon Gropius,
the angel he loved
beyond the tribute of a violin.

The wasp's sting turned septic,
a fistula in the bowel,
medical cure unavailable.

Slowly, Wozzeck, one thing after another.

Slowly, his fifty years slipped from his hand.

THE CLIMB

His eyes fill with wonder
as he has known at night
when the stars seem
inside his head.
Flowers begin to swarm in the air,
and he flows

like a breath through a wind instrument –
a sweet note played to the gods.
Gods have no path;
but they hear:
in this resonant void
he *is*.

JOHANN STRAUSS

Four hundred violins sent heaven
to earth. Fanning their faces to three-four time,
the corset too tight,
some women fainted.

The Blue Danube begins –
waves turn to gold
keep rolling
and rolling.

His second marriage ending in divorce,
as a Catholic not allowed to remarry,
he became a Protestant and a Saxon national –
he, the most Austrian of composers

golden in the Stadtpark:
encircled by naked muses floating on stone.
A baton is lifted,
the river flows, always flows.

INFATUATION

After her divorce
she heard that Johann Strauß
was coming to Boston to give a concert
at the Coliseum.

She flew into a fever,
put on her sequinned gown,
queued with other Boston women
paying a hundred dollars each

for a lock of the maestro's hair
his servant had cut
from several black poodles
to fulfill the demand of these groupies.

Then off to the ball for a chance
to dance with the king of waltz
(who himself couldn't dance).
Her soft, rocking breath: *Divine!* –

body perfectly tuned
to her partner's rhythm.
Powdering her face
she made light of the dismal weather

to anyone inferring her marriage
should never have happened,
rejoiced in her ease;
danced away her married name

into the small hours.
The king of waltz had not shown up.
She slept with his black lock
beside her on the pillow.

COMPOSING

At Rose Lake in Senegal
a miracle happened at midday:
the water turned pink in the sun.

Translucent glow, like of a breast,
compassionate pink, generously given,
quickly withdrawn.

The days are shortening in England.
A wren's satellite song
needles at the north window.

He moves through the house
to the south to catch that same
compassionate pink

wrapping the horizon;
sits down at the piano
and continents swing round.

Tapping the keys he savours
each sound as if it were
a berry placed in his mouth

and to bite or swallow
were sacrilegious.
The memory of a frog

plunging into Rose Lake – *Plop!* –
and now the wings of an owl
caressing the yew-hedge

and still that singular *Plop!*
into the chill that hangs at the south window
offering itself to a dark god.

MUSIC FOR THOUGHT

Her beauty of younger years
lured by the piano-play
she listens to;

back turned to the pianist conjuring
a fountain of melodies she's almost forgotten.
With melancholy seriousness

he peers at the diners' nest of food,
their conversing eyes.
There, a glint of recognition, like an egg

cracking in warmth.
He can see only the back of her head,
but a movement in her shoulders,

a run of emotion,
tells him she's with him.
In his music she scatters into islands;

in his music, the islands rejoin.
He feeds her tune after tune:
a dazzling secret

as he switches keys.
His foolish goodness
shines in and through her –

her face, a warm sea,
endures its own drowning.

FRANZ LISZT AT THE VILLA D'ESTE

His thoughts revolved around
the relic of St. Catherine's hand
he'd seen in Rome. Long, slender
fingers in the music of air.

At the Trevi fountain
he flipped a coin
over his shoulder
to land among all others in the water.

When he stayed at the Villa d'Este,
the fountains at once
sprang to life,
talked, cried,

entered his imagination,
took him to new heights;
fingerprints of the divine
on the pool's querulous face;

spray, trickle
becoming a piano-score,
for days he bent to its course –
until it was music never heard before.

ATTEMPT AT REVISING A MUSICAL SCORE

The score you've written
does not match what you heard
in your inner ear.

Trying to pinpoint your failure
is like being deep in the woods:
there's nothing

and yet you feel as in a dream
meeting something wild
and being equal to it.

A hint of presence –
moving stealthily
listening to you.

MESSIAEN'S CREATURES

At thirty-two degrees centigrade
the bats came in through the window,
shadow-danced around his bed
where he watched their flirtation
with the night.

On a June day
he walked along fields
when from all sides
swallows brushed against his sleeves,
swooped and turned

and in all this movement
he stood still,
mesmerised by these avian creatures
who seemed to lift him
up in the air.

The bats came again as he lay with failing health,
brought chance messages,
played with the roof over his head,
with his inventory of memories –
vanished with his stare.

CHILD'S PLAY

(after a song by Mozart)

Come, let's have fun! Those windows
have been shuttered for years.
The balustrade rusty from many winters,
door bolted and double-locked.

Let's break in! Let's have a picnic in there
with drink and smoking, thinking of girls
and the owner in a hundred year slumber.
Let's kick the pots with dead plants,

pull out what's hidden in cupboards and drawers –
we're only young: can roll in the hay
afterwards. No harm will come.
We'll laugh at those skeletons poking from closets –

and when the sun goes down,
too early, as always, we'll have tomorrow
to run and run, be lost
and found in another story.

ROCK

A lonely road into French hills.
It is dusk. He drives so fast,
keeping his foot down even on
bends, mocking that sudden
spark of fear – but really the fear is singing,
and he marvels at how smooth the wheels
grip – like gliding over the shell of an egg.

What lies beyond the windscreen
has neither beginning nor end.
We'll rock around the clock, he sings,
and then her way of cracking an egg
comes into his mind, rolling the yolk
from one severed half
to the other, the white rocking in the bowl.

Speed. Danger. Being in control,
being his own man, his own master –
steely and vocal;
her stirring the yolk into the dough –
the moment something in him
starts to confess: watch how soon
it turns into a lie that steers him home.

PRESENCE

Nowhere to escape the maid,
ill in bed, she watched her polish the silver:

sunlight wobbled on the ceiling
as if God were playing with a thread.

She saw her bee-wax, dust and tidy –
charming something serious

into existence.
And yet she did not want her presence:

did not want being witnessed;
even when the maid wiped the mirror,

then quietly shut the door,
she knew she was not alone.

Later, living in a care-home,
she was surrounded by several

of different heights and smiles,
wheeling her to a sunny patch.

She opened an inner window;
drifted away playing the piano,

the organ, the trumpet, the saxophone –
the sun bathed what survived of her.

RELEASED

(after a song by Richard Strauss)

You will not cry when I keep
repeating myself. It happens at my age.
You will smile at my anecdote
you've heard many times –
I'll give it to you like a kiss on the journey –
what happiness!

The same phrase will creep
into my talk – I won't notice it.
Then it will be a single word
I can't get out of my mind:
When, or *Help*, or *Mother*.
You will stroke my hand – what happiness!

It's all right, you'll say. And I will
search your face: perhaps in your eyes
will see something inside me burst
and I'll say *My love* –
still to remember that –
oh, what happiness!

FOUND TICKET

On a January morning
a partial eclipse of the sun.
Day shrank into doorways.

As the moon released the cabbage-sun
I saw a ticket in the gutter:
a cello concert with Rostropovich.

To hear classical music live for the first time!
Apprehensive at being a finder and keeper
I sat in the gods of Vienna's Konzerthaus.

Rostropovich took up position.
It was the late 1960s. Soon the Russians
were to invade Prague.

A web of sounds
that could have
rocked in a sunlit breeze,

and in each my tears.
Like a nocturnal bird
Rostropovich glided with his bow,

emptied our minds of thought.
Walking home under moon and stars
there was *love*, even in drawn curtains.

ECHOING

In a pasture
he blows the alpenhorn –

a deep, plump sound
echoing from the mountains.

In 1890s Budapest
an opera was relayed

down telephone lines

and his Parkinson-struck great-great uncle
inwardly sang

to a blaze of love,
duplicity, intrigue,

to that single note
on the triangle.

NOCTURNE

In the stable after dusk
sitting on a pile of straw
in the company of horses;

waiting for night –
a bride taking off her gown;
the air soft and calm.

It begins with the moon –
a face in the moon –
the dead listening.

COMA

(after Richard Strauss's "Four Last Songs")

I

I saw you sink onto the paving stones
by the gate. It was there
our journey out of time began.
You fell into something so deep,
as if night itself
had taken you.

I sat by your bed, spoke your name,
imagined my voice an angel
touching your skin,
mentioning familiar things.
Once, your face, lit by sun,
lay like a miracle before me.

Somewhere far off
you were light itself, beckoning me
to come into your infinity.
I trembled at this death in you
that took gigantic form,
yet was so calm, so tender, so blessed.

II

The garden is mourning you.
I chopped down the Michaelmas daisies.
September – six months
in which your countenance hasn't changed.

Sometimes the errand-scent of your aftershave
meets me in the hall. I'm part of your sleep,
wandering through rooms
in a circle of memory.

The roses you smelled:
closing your eyes, longing for peace.
That peace has taken you like lightning.
And now you sleep, neither in this world, nor in the next.

III

I keep vigil by your bed.
Whisper your name; my voice rising a notch,
anticipating yours. I stroke your hand
as if I were gazing

into a deep lake, not surprised
that it reflects nothing but my own face.
The days are wearying. Like an exhausted
child, I long for sleep;

for sleep that is like a deep current
in the ocean; perhaps there
we will join hands: you'll see my face,
and we'll delight in what has been absent for so long.

IV

We've gone through thick and thin.
All day I looked into a dark
and musty place where flowers
we'd grown through many seasons

hung dried and bunched from walls.
Can you see them too?
Can you see the larks
rising in the air

where we gathered red campion and feverfew?
Come back and let them soar once more.
Let us not lose ourselves: you in your sleep,
I in my sorrow.

Such vast stillness is enfolding us.
The clouds are giving way to a crimson sun.
A fiery curtain opens for a golden ray;
then the horizon's desire to go further

is wiped out.